CW00404797

Bradwell's Pocket Walking Guides

The
Yorkshire
Dales

BRADWELL
BOOKS

Published by Bradwell Books

9 Orgreave Close Sheffield S13 9NP

Email: books@bradwellbooks.co.uk

British Library Cataloguing in Publication Data: a catalogue record for this book is available from the British Library.

1st Edition

ISBN: 9781910551943

Extracts edited by: Louise Maskill

Design, typesetting and mapping: Mark Titterton

Photograph credits: iStock - Front Cover; Mark Titterton - p.15

Print: Gomer Press, Llandysul, Ceredigion SA44 4JL

Maps contain Ordnance Survey data

CONTENTS

FACT FILE & INTRODUCTION

FACT FILE

The information in the walk descriptions is produced in good faith, and should be adequate to get you from start to finish, but it is always advisable to take a relevant Ordnance Survey map with you. The correct maps for each walk are recommended in 'The Essentials' sections – OS Explorer maps are highly detailed maps of a relatively small area (1:25,000 scale, 4cm on the map equals 1km on the ground), while the OS Landranger series are less detailed (1:50,000 scale, 2cm on the map equals 1km on the ground) but show a larger area per map. For these walks the Landranger maps are adequate, but the Explorer maps are more precise – the choice is yours.

All the walks in this book follow rights of way or paths open to the public, with occasional roadside paths (take care when crossing roads). The walks should be suitable for most people, especially families, ranging in length from around 3 to 5 miles. They are graded and described in 'The Essentials' sections to help you select the most appropriate walk for your party. Walking boots are recommended for all walks, with plenty of insulating layers of clothing and a waterproof jacket and overtrousers if indicated by the weather forecast.

Locations for purchasing refreshments are suggested in 'The Essentials' sections, but are usually located at the start and end points of the walks, so packing a drink and a snack for your walk is advisable. Take advantage of public toilets where available!

By law, dogs must be kept on a lead wherever there is livestock, as well as in moorland areas during nesting season and where sheep roam freely. They should also be on a lead if they are likely to be a nuisance to other walkers or cyclists, and certainly when crossing roads. **You should be sure that your dog can manage to get over stiles before you set off on any of these walks; see 'Route' in 'The Essentials' to check whether there are any stiles on the walk you would like to undertake.**

Bradwell Books and the authors have made all reasonable efforts to ensure that the details are correct at the time of publication. Bradwell Books and the authors cannot accept responsibility for any changes that have taken place subsequent to the book being published. It is the responsibility of individuals undertaking any of the walks listed in this book to exercise due care and consideration for their own health and wellbeing and that of others in their party. The walks in this book are not especially strenuous, but individuals taking part should ensure they are fit and well before setting off.

INTRODUCTION

The Yorkshire Dales form one of England's premier destinations. The majority of the area was designated a National Park in 1954, with this upland landscape at the very heart of the mighty Pennine chain stretching from Hadrian's Wall in the north to the Peak District in the south.

This beautiful area consists of a string of valleys divided by high and lonely moorlands. Although there are literally scores of 'dales in the Dales', the principal valleys are Wensleydale, Wharfedale and Swaledale, ably supported by Nidderdale, Malhamdale, Ribblesdale and Dentdale. It is perhaps the villages that best portray the real feel of the Dales, with Burnsall, Muker, Dent and Bainbridge representing some of England's finest. A string of such villages is ranged at regular intervals along every valley, each one different yet all looking as if they grew out of the very land. Their charm is further enhanced by their setting, as neatly packaged fields and rolling fells form a perfect backdrop.

Second only to the villages are the waterfalls. Every dale has some, from the lofty plunge of Hardraw Force and the celebrated trio at Aysgarth to countless smaller gems hidden in folds of the hills. In this book there's even an entire walk dedicated to Ingleton's splendid collection.

The past is never far away in the Dales; the eastern half of the region boasts several castles and abbeys, while more recent history is evident in the lead-mining industry that employed thousands of dalesmen less than two hundred years ago. Naturally, farming plays a crucial role in maintaining the countryside as we always picture it, with sheep and cattle grazing among field barns, drystone walls, hay meadows and upland pasture. Most villages offer a welcoming pub or tearoom, and other attractions include visitor centres, show caves and folk museums. Additionally, all manner of local crafts can be experienced, including cheesemaking, ropemaking and brewing. When a little more bustle is required, the area is conveniently surrounded by a necklace of gateway towns of varying sizes such as Skipton, Richmond, Harrogate and Ilkley.

The call of the Dales is one that begs to be answered, and you won't be disappointed!

1. INGLETON

THE ESSENTIALS

Distance: 4½ miles (7.2 km)

Route: Quite demanding; numerous minor ups and downs. One stile

Time: Approx. 3 hours

Terrain: Mostly firm well-made paths; can be muddy though

Starting Point: Waterfalls Trail in Ingleton. Grid ref SD 693 733; postcode LA6 3ES. Note that this walk is over private land, and requires payment at the start

Parking: Waterfalls Trail car park, as above

Food and Toilets: Café at start, refreshments at Beezleys part-way round. Public toilets at start

Maps: OS Explorer 2 (Yorkshire Dales South/West); OS Landranger 98 (Wensleydale and Upper Wharfedale)

INTRODUCTION

Ingleton is at the heart of Yorkshire's limestone country, and makes an ideal base for exploring the fells, scars, caves and valleys. The centre is dominated by a long-abandoned railway viaduct and St Mary's Church, but there are numerous interesting little corners. The youth hostel is centrally situated, as are pubs, cafés and shops. There is also a climbing wall and a heated, open-air swimming pool.

The Waterfalls Walk is one of two very famous walking excursions from Ingleton, the other being an ascent of its hill, Ingleborough. The falls walk has attracted visitors for over a century, and can be worth savouring in the winter months when it si quieter. The paths are well maintained – justifying the charge – but care is still needed when wet leaves carpet the ground or in wintry conditions. You should also be aware that for a low-level walk, there is a fair amount of 'up and down' work.

The walk passes through the valley of the River Twiss before briefly crossing more open surrounds to return by the near-parallel valley of the River Doe. These two dales are remarkably alike, each wooded and with some fascinating geological features, particularly the Craven Fault. In fact, even without its waterfalls this would still be a fine stroll. Immediately below the walk's starting point in Ingleton the two streams meet to form the River Greta, which goes on to join the Lune. Of the many waterfalls encountered, Thornton Force is head and shoulders above the rest – a massive tumble of water in a colourful setting.

The western stream, the Twiss, begins life as Kingsdale Beck in a beautifully unfrequented limestone valley immediately upstream between the mountains of Whernside and Gragareth. The flat valley floor of Kingsdale was occupied by a glacial lake held back by Raven Ray, a good example of a moraine, which you encounter just above Thornton Force. The River Doe starts out in Chapel-le-Dale, running another level course between the mountains of Whernside and Ingleborough. The latter peak forms a fine backdrop to the central part of this walk as you transfer from one valley to the other.

1. INGLETON WALK

ROUTE

1. Few directions
    are needed
    as the paths
    are very clear
    throughout,
    and the way is
    obvious. From
    the car park
    the path heads
    up the valley of
    the Twiss, twice
    crossing the river
    above Swilla
    Glen (at Manor
    Bridge and Pecca
    Bridge) to arrive
    at Pecca Falls.

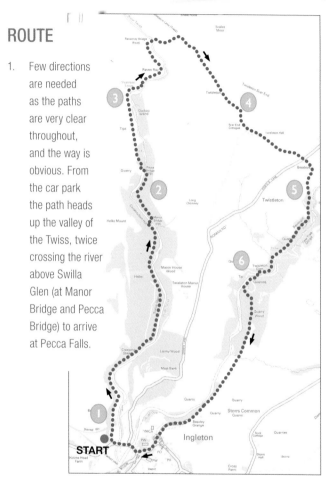

2. Some steeper work leads up past Hollybush Spout and more
    open country follows, passing an old refreshment hut to
    reach the walk's highlight at Thornton Force. Few will not
    take a rest here at this major highlight of the walk.

3. Above it, another bridge takes the path up a steep field and onto Twisleton Lane. Turn right along its green course, which becomes surfaced on dropping down to Twisleton Hall.

4. Here, bear left on a track passing above all the buildings and on through a stile at the end. A good path crosses the field and descends to a gate onto a back road. Fine views to Ingleborough dominate this section of the walk. Cross straight over to Beezleys Farm, passing between the buildings to a gate on the left. The Falls Refreshment Centre awaits, open seasonally and at weekends.

5. Drop down to Beezley Falls and follow the River Doe back downstream. Features along the way include Rival Falls, a dramatic viewing platform above Baxengill Gorge, the easily missed Snow Falls, and only one crossing of the beck.

6. Emerging from the trees high above the river at Cat Leap Fall, the path runs on by old quarry remains on the lower slopes of Storrs Common. This final section enjoys an interesting prospect of the striking tilted rock strata in the old quarry across the beck. At the end a road-end is met to lead along to the village, joining the main street then dropping steeply down past the church to finish.

2. SETTLE

THE ESSENTIALS

Distance: 3¾ miles (6 km)

Route: Easy; one short climb to Langcliffe, and one steep field above. Some gates, five stiles

Time: Approx. 2 hours

Terrain: Mostly fieldpaths

Starting Point: Market Place, Settle town centre. Grid ref SD 819 636, postcode BD24 9EJ

Parking: Central car parks in Settle

Food and Toilets: Pubs, cafés and public toilets near start

Maps: OS Explorer 2 (Yorkshire Dales South/West); OS Landranger 98 (Wensleydale and Upper Wharfedale)

INTRODUCTION

The bustling little town of Settle is an important focal point for an extensive rural area extending beyond upper Ribblesdale. It is invariably busy, being a long-established halting place for those bound further afield, and also ideally centred for the Three Peaks district.

Market days present the liveliest scene, when each Tuesday the small square is awash with colour. Shops, pubs and cafés are interspersed between numerous interesting old buildings. Facing the square is the historic row known as The Shambles, with shops peeping from behind archways. Nearby is the Folly, a rambling seventeenth century house with a spectacularly intricate facade. The Museum of North Craven Life gives a rewarding insight into the district's past, while the limestone cliff of Castleberg provides a dramatic bird's-eye view of the town today. Also facing the square is a former inn, 'Ye Olde Naked Man', its carved sign dated 1633 and well placed to spare his blushes. The church of the Holy Ascension stands at the northern end of town and dates from 1838. Also of note are the Town Hall (1833), Victoria Hall (1853) and the Friends' Meeting House (1689). Also, of course, there is always the railway, with the famous Settle-Carlisle line beginning its journey through the Dales.

Stackhouse is a cosy grouping of exclusive dwellings huddled beneath the hillside, and appears happy to remain hidden in its protective greenery. The River Ribble at nearby Locks is a good place to appraise nineteenth-century Dales industry: from the footbridge you look down on the weir that supplied the adjacent millpond which provided water for the large mill at the other end, while alongside you are two rows of cottages that would once have been occupied by workers at the mill.

Langcliffe is a delightful village spread alongside a spacious green. Opposite the phone box where you enter the village, look for a tablet on a house wall depicting the Naked Woman, modestly dated 1660; once an inn, it was a close friend of Settle's more famous Naked Man. The church of St John the Evangelist overlooks the green, while assorted lovely old cottages sit back from the war memorial fountain. The walk's return route gives a panoramic picture back over the village with Ingleborough beyond, while up-dale, Pen-y-ghent overtops the limestone of Stainforth Scar.

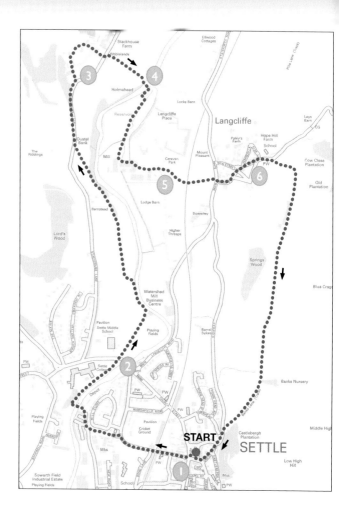

ROUTE

1. From the Town Hall, cross the main road and head down Kirkgate, passing the Friends' Meeting House. Under the railway bridge keep ahead, and at the bend leave the road and take a footway left of the fire station. At the end swing right around the back of Kings Mill. Go left to a footbridge over the Ribble and walk upstream to Settle Bridge.

2. Cross the road and head straight off along an enclosed path between sports fields. At the end join the river briefly before turning into a field. Cross to a prominent gap-stile and follow the path above a steep wooded riverbank. Emerging again, bear left to a stile just beyond a gate onto Stackhouse Lane. Turn right to the edge of Stackhouse.

3. A short loop gives a slightly closer look at Stackhouse: take the first rough road into it, turning first right along what becomes a grassy track, then right again back to the road. A few strides further on, take a walled path right alongside a solitary house at Ribblelands. This meets the Ribble at Locks.

4. Cross the footbridge and turn right along a narrow street between millworkers' cottages. At the end a short path runs left to a former millpond. Turn right on the path running the full length of this pond. At the end the path swings left between pond and mill to meet an access road. Go left on this as far as the junction ahead, alongside Langcliffe Park caravan site.

2. SETTLE WALK

5. Go straight ahead on a walled path, rising to cross the railway and to the valley road at Langcliffe. Cross to an old lane opposite and into the village centre. Emerging onto the green, remain on the road past the fountain and between the old school on the left and the church on the right.

6. As the road leaves the village, passing through a gateway prior to climbing, instead take a gate to the right. A path ascends steeply to a gate at the top. Bear right from here on a lower path above a wall, now levelling out. Beyond a bridlegate, advance to a gate by converging walls to merge with another bridleway from the left. Following a wall to a gate at the end, Banks Lane descends onto a back lane at the top of Constitution Hill. Turn left to return to the centre.

Janet's Foss waterfall, Gordale Beck - Malham Walk   (© Mark Titterton)

3. MALHAM

THE ESSENTIALS

Distance: 4½ miles (7.2 km)

Route: Easy; a short, steep climb above Gordale Bridge, and care needed on limestone pavement and during a steep, stepped descent from the Cove. Several gates, one stile

Time: Approx. 2½ to 3 hours

Terrain: Mostly firm paths, also a limestone pavement

Starting Point: Malham village centre.
Grid ref SD 900 626, postcode BD23 4DG

Parking: National Park car park, as above

Food and Toilets: Pubs and cafés in village; refreshment van often at Gordale. Public toilets near the start

Maps: OS Explorer 2 (Yorkshire Dales South/West);
OS Landranger 98 (Wensleydale and Upper Wharfedale)

INTRODUCTION

Malhamdale is the name given to the opening miles of the River Aire. Though not one of the Dales' major rivers, the Aire begins here in limestone country before heading for Skipton and the towns and cities of West Yorkshire.

The beating heart of Malhamdale is tiny Malham village, a busy spot with attractive seventeenth and eighteenth century cottages. The Lister Arms dates from 1723 and bears the arms of the Lords Ribblesdale, while the Buck Inn and cafés offer further refreshment. In monastic times the religious houses of Bolton Priory and Fountains Abbey owned much of the land hereabouts, with reminders in the names of two of Malham's bridges, Monk

Bridge and Prior Moon's clapper bridge. A National Park Centre stands by the car park, and the village also has a popular youth hostel astride the Pennine Way.

The beautiful waterfall of Janet's Foss shelters in a wooded hollow, and somehow seems the archetypal Dales waterfall. Its woods are a rich habitat for flora and fauna, though there is little to better the springtime aroma of wild garlic that carpets the woodland floor. Meanwhile Gordale Scar, a colossal limestone ravine, is probably the most awe-inspiring feature of the Yorkshire Dales. The grandeur of its overhanging cliffs can initially be too daunting to appreciate the waterfalls formed by Gordale Beck: the upper one spills spectacularly through a circular hole in the rocks.

Malham Cove is another iconic Dales landmark: half a mile north of the village, it forms a sheer limestone cliff rising some 300 feet (90 metres) from the valley floor. It is hard to imagine the waterfall that once plunged over here after its journey down the Dry Valley immediately above. The top of the Cove comprises an extensive limestone pavement that is fascinating to tread, but take care as the 'grikes' in between could easily snap a misplaced leg.

In springtime climbers share the Cove walls with peregrine falcons that have nested here for many years; an RSPB observation post is usually sited on the Cove approach path. Issuing from the base of the Cove is Malham Beck, which sank below ground on the moors above. At Aire Head Springs below the village it is united with other previously subterranean waters to form the 'official' birthplace of the River Aire.

3. MALHAM WALK

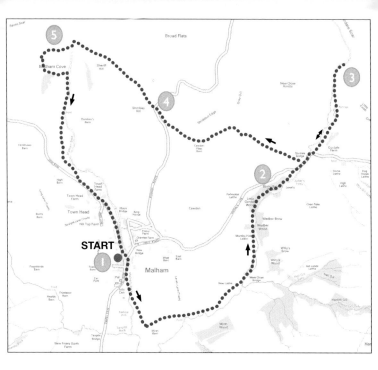

ROUTE

1. Head into the village, crossing Malham Beck at a footbridge by the forge. Turn downstream on a short lane, becoming a path to a bridlegate. From here a broad path crosses a couple of fields, veering away from the beck. At a kissing gate the Pennine Way goes straight ahead, but your path swings left to a barn and continues through several kissing gates along the near side of Gordale Beck. When the beck appears properly, follow it upstream on a flagged section; a pasture leads to a kissing gate into a section of woodland and the charming waterfall of Janet's Foss.

2. Here the path breaks left to emerge onto the road to Gordale. Turn right for a short distance, passing a refreshment van which is often near the old bridge and its modern replacement. The walk returns to this point after visiting Gordale Scar. A short distance further on is Gordale House; a gate on the left leads to a well-trodden path towards the unmistakable cliffs of Gordale Scar, which converge as you enter the ravine to view the waterfalls.

3. Return to the old bridge; a kissing gate on your right leads to a firm path rising to a wall corner. A grassy path climbs to a gate, then slants to another at the top corner. A firm path runs along to the left along a wall, which drops away to reveal Malham village below and Pendle Hill beyond. Your path swings gently right to rise parallel with the Malham Tarn road before joining it at a kissing gate.

4. Cross to a stile, from where a track heads across the pasture. This follows a near-level course above a wall to reach a wall corner ahead. When the wall turns away, the route forks; the right branch rises to a stile ahead, but your way bears down and left, with the limestone pavement at the top of Malham Cove immediately below. Drop to a bridlegate in a wall to access the top of the Cove.

5. Taking great care, cross to the far side of the pavement where a kissing gate leads to some four hundred steps down to the end of the Cove. At the bottom, bear left across the base of the cliff, with Malham Beck issuing from it. To return to Malham, turn downstream on a path through fields to emerge on the road on the edge of the village.

4. REETH

INTRODUCTION

Swaledale is at its most colourful and vibrant around Reeth, where the major side valley of Arkengarthdale joins the Swale in the shadow of the long, high skyline of Fremington Edge. Additionally, Harkerside Moor dominates the main dale across the river.

Reeth is the heart of Swaledale. It boasts an enviable position on the slopes of Calver Hill, well above the confluence of the Swale and Arkle Beck. A large, sloping green is central, with the main buildings standing back on all sides. This old market town exudes a confident air, with ancient inns, shops and tearooms alongside the green; there is also a National Park Centre. Parking limitations can result in an untidy scene around the green in summer, aggravated when market traders set up stalls on

Fridays. Historically linked with the lead mining industry, Reeth was once much more populous. There is an absorbing folk museum, while annual agricultural shows and festivals add to the town's cultural attractions.

Grinton, the only settlement of any size on the south bank of the Swale, was once the major centre for the dale above Richmond. At the centre are a pub, a church, and a Literary Institute dating from 1903. St Andrew's Church is known as the 'Cathedral of the Dales' because of its size. Until a chapel was established at Muker, its parish extended through the entire valley as far as the Westmorland border. As this was the only consecrated ground prior to 1580, the deceased of the upper dale had to be carried on a long and arduous journey down a path known today as the 'corpse road'. Between the church and the river is Blackburn Hall, a manor house with sections believed to be much older than its 1635 datestone.

Either side of Grinton the River Swale itself takes centre stage; its riverside paths are a delight to tread. The tiny settlement of Fremington is divided into two halves; Low Fremington is by the main road, while High Fremington is a haphazard grouping of dwellings with enviable privacy linked by a network of narrow byways.

4. REETH WALK

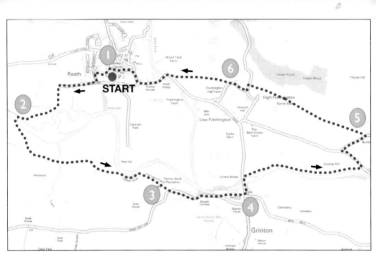

ROUTE

1. From the green walk in front of the Kings Arms and the Black Bull to another tiny green at Anvil Square. Across it, set back to the right, a sign directs 'To the river' along a path between walls. It emerges onto a narrow road: go left to a suburban street. Turn left to a T-junction, then right along a lane past the surgery. At the end, turn left down an enclosed footway to a gate overlooking the river. The path bears right through two fields to cross a suspension footbridge over the Swale.

2. On the other side of the river, turn downstream on a grassy bank which diverts from the river's course. At a corner, turn left on a bridleway that passes through a gate, then to a corner gate, where it becomes enclosed and eventually rejoins the Swale. As the river veers off again the path resumes its course, bearing right to a gate onto a back road.

3. Go left towards Grinton, and after the church tower appears, follow a path left down steps to the riverbank. Pass the churchyard and emerge onto an access road, passing Blackburn Hall to reach into the village centre opposite the Bridge Inn.

4. Go left to cross the bridge, then turn downstream on a path which eventually emerges into open pasture. At the other end a wooded bank leads up to a stile onto the Marrick Priory access road. Turn left to a through road, then right for a few uphill minutes to a gap-stile on the left just before a driveway.

5. Cross to a stile in the left corner ahead, then follow the wall and go through a gate to its other side. Go through two further gates and follow a fence above Sorrel Sykes Farm to an enclosed way. Ignore this, going through a gate ahead to follow a wallside path to a small gate and an enclosed footway on the edge of Fremington. Head along the path to a narrow lane, following it left and then first right.

6. The lane swings left to drop steeply away; here, go ahead on a short track to a gate into a field. The track soon bears right, but you need to follow a path tracing the left-hand wall down to a corner stile, then down again to cross a stile. Aiming for Reeth Bridge, cross the field to a gate. Another just beyond brings you to the bridge road over Arkle Beck. Cross to re-enter the village, passing a corner shop to rise back onto the green.

5. HARDRAW

THE ESSENTIALS

Distance: 4½ miles (7.2 km)

Route: Medium; mostly easy, but steep climb through four fields to Sedbusk. Over 20 stiles, but many of these can be avoided by using Sedbusk Lane where indicated in the route description

Time: Approx. 3 hours

Terrain: Almost entirely grassy, sometimes stone-flagged fieldpaths

Starting Point: National Park Centre, Hawes town centre. Grid ref SD 875 899, postcode DL8 3NT

Parking: Pay and display in National Park car park, as above

Food and Toilets: Pubs and cafés at start; pub and tearoom at Hardraw. Public toilets at start

Maps: OS Explorer 30 (Yorkshire Dales North/Central); OS Landranger 98 (Wensleydale and Upper Wharfedale)

INTRODUCTION

Upper Wensleydale is hemmed in by high and extensive fells, but at Hawes it broadens out into an arrangement of green pastures where sheep and cattle graze to their hearts' content. Though not as dramatic as some of the dales, its sedate appearance hides old villages and impressive waterfalls, as well as a string of side valleys along its southern flank.

Hardraw is a tiny hamlet made famous by its waterfall, claimed to be the highest single drop above ground in England. It also has a church, St Mary and St John, and a tearoom. Access to Hardraw Force is through the Green Dragon inn, where a charge is made to view the 'private' spectacle; it is a five-minute walk into the impressive amphitheatre. The cliff over which the water spills is Hardraw Scaur, or Scar. In the gorge below the force band contests take place each September – the bandstand is passed on the way.

Hawes is the 'capital' of upper Wensleydale, and retains an unconventional layout well worth a leisurely exploration. This lively market town gains even greater character during its Tuesday market, when there are as many locals in evidence as there are tourists. Once the last stop on the Wensleydale branch line, its former station is now the Dales Countryside Museum, where one can learn of local life and industry of the not-so-distant past, with a National Park Centre alongside.

Two surviving industries are today also tourist attractions. The ropemakers is also by the old station, where you can observe and purchase any number of associated products. The creamery is a long-established business that was on the verge of disappearing in 1992; these days, however, it is a hugely popular attraction that offers a 'must-do' experience. Milk from the cows you might see on your walk is used in the production of the celebrated Wensleydale cheese: from watching the cows munch the grass to nibbling the finished product, you can enjoy the whole experience!

The high point of your walk is the unspoiled hamlet of Sedbusk, whose farms and cottages look across the dale to Hawes and beyond from an altitude of a little under 1,000 feet (300 metres). It is so laid back it has even avoided the back road from Hardraw to Askrigg, being reached only by a narrow lane.

5. HARDRAW WALK

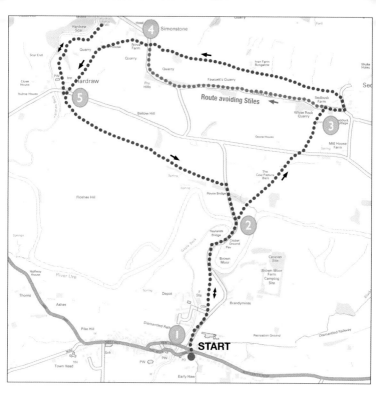

ROUTE

1. Leave the car park on a path climbing to the road. Turn right over the bridge and out of town on a footway. Soon a kissing-gate marks the Pennine Way; follow its flagged course to rejoin the road a little further on. Cross Haylands Bridge over the River Ure, then take a stile on the right, crossing the field to a stone-arched bridge.

2. From the bridge a path climbs half-right to a stile on the brow, from where a flagged path ascends a field to a stile in the top

corner. Cross the road to a stile opposite, and continue ahead to a stile ahead. Dropping to a stile just below, climb steeply past a barn to another stile in the top-right corner. Emerge onto Sedbusk Lane. *To avoid around a dozen stiles, turn left on this byway, turning right at the end to pick up the main route at Simonstone*. Otherwise, turn right to Sedbusk. At a junction by a Victorian postbox turn left to enter the village.

3. Head up the lane between houses. Part-way along, go left across the green to a gap, and on between houses to emerge into a field. Follow the path straight ahead, along a distinct shelf across fields connected by a series of gap-stiles. Passing barns, continue straight on; the only ladder-stile can be avoided through an adjacent gate as you approach a second cluster of barns. Pass along behind and out onto the road through Simonstone.

4. After a short distance, turn right on an access road to the front of Simonstone Hall. Go over a stile on the left, crossing the field top outside the gardens to a stile. The path crosses to West House Farm; go between the buildings to a stile, then left to reveal Hardraw immediately below. Drop to a stile by a covered reservoir; a path descends a steep field. Pass through a small enclosure and a yard to emerge on the street alongside the pub. To visit Hardraw Force pay a fee at the pub, from where a well-made path follows Hardraw Beck upstream past a bandstand to the waterfall.

5. Back on the road, opposite the pub take a track left of the bridge to a kissing-gate, from where a path sets off left through the fields, crossing several stiles. At a gateway, keep ahead to a kissing-gate at the end, then advance along the bottom edge of two fields to a small gate onto a road. Turn right, descending to pick up the route over Haylands Bridge and back into Hawes.

6. AYSGARTH FALLS

THE ESSENTIALS

Distance: 3¼ miles (5.2 km)

Route: Easy; mostly level, but short pull near start. Twelve stiles

Time: Approx. 2 hours

Terrain: Riverbank and fieldpaths

Starting Point: Aysgarth Falls, east of village.
Grid ref SE 012 888, postcode DL8 3TH

Parking: Pay and display in National Park car park, as above

Food and Toilets: Café at start; further café and pub in village close to start. Public toilets at start

Maps: OS Explorer 30 (Yorkshire Dales North/Central);
OS Landranger 98 (Wensleydale and Upper Wharfedale)

INTRODUCTION

The broad green valley of Wensleydale is perhaps best known for its waterfalls, which occur not only on the River Ure itself but also in several of its many side valleys. The spectacular drop of Hardraw Force is visited in the Hawes walk, while this excursion takes you to the equally celebrated Aysgarth Falls on the Ure itself.

Aysgarth's arrangement of Upper, Middle and Lower Falls are spread along a short mile's length of the river. All the falls are very similar in nature as the Ure tumbles over the Yoredale Series of limestone rocks to create a water wonderland. The Upper Falls (High Force on maps) are the most commonly viewed, being immediately upstream of Yore Bridge at the very start. The Middle Falls (Middle Force) are only marginally more distant, a short way downstream of the bridge and seen from a viewing platform at the end of the walk. On this walk the Lower Falls (Lower Force) are viewed from the less-visited south bank of the river, and an even lower waterfall is also visited.

The spectacular river scenery at Aysgarth is massively enhanced by the setting – the lovely glades of Freeholders' Wood on the north bank boast carpets of springtime flowers and rich birdlife. Yore is the old name for Ure, and it crops up regularly hereabouts, most notably at the former spinning mill of Yore Mill, currently a café and gift shop next to Yore Bridge.

Set in spacious grounds, the enormous (by Dales standards) St Andrew's Church was restored in the nineteenth century, with only the tower base remaining from medieval times. Its finest feature is inside, in the shape of two superb fifteenth and sixteenth century screens. Aysgarth village itself stands half a mile to the west, with the George and Dragon pub, a tearoom and a pleasant green, as well as an intriguing Edwardian rock garden and a Quaker burial ground.

6. AYSGARTH FALLS WALK

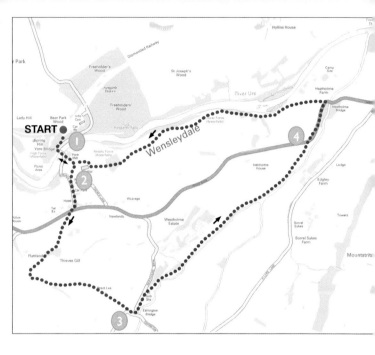

ROUTE

1. From the far end of the car park a path runs down to Yore Bridge, viewpoint for the Upper Falls. At its corner a path climbs to enter St Andrew's churchyard.

2. Follow the church path right to the road, and climb past the Falls café-bar to a junction at the Aysgarth Falls Hotel. Cross to a stile and bear right across the field, crossing a farm access road to a wall-stile opposite. Continue ahead to a small gate in a fence, then bear right to a gate leading into a small wood. A path drops through it, then heads along the base of a shallow valley. At a path crossroads, turn left

through a stile by an old gate, and head away through a minor nick. Instead of following the broader path ahead, take a narrow path left to a stile. Head to a gate left of some trees, then down a larger field to a gate near the bottom of the opposite wall. Drop down through a gate right of a barn, then steeply down to a stile below, continuing to another onto a narrow lane. Go left to the road at Eshington Bridge.

3. Without crossing, go straight over onto a path downstream with Bishopdale Beck, passing wooden lodges at Westholme. Continue to pass an attractive confluence with Walden Beck, with Bolton Castle visible ahead. After some open pasture you reach a stile onto the A684. Go right to approach Hestholme Bridge, but without crossing turn left at Hestholme's drive.

4. From a gate on the left cross to the far corner to a wooded bank above the Ure. Turn upstream on a good path, meeting the riverbank at a long, low waterfall. At a stile beyond the path rises up above a wooded bank, to continue higher above. Through a small gate there are splendid views of Aysgarth's Lower Falls. The path remains high along a fence above the falls, goes through a further gate, and climbs higher above a steeper bank. With the Middle Falls visible ahead, bear left with a fence to a wood corner; a stile leads to a path through the trees, emerging with the church ahead. Cross the field to the churchyard to retrace your steps to the start. By remaining on the road after the bridge you reach a gate on the right, leading to a short path downstream through Freeholders' Wood to view the Middle Falls more closely.

7. BOLTON CASTLE

THE ESSENTIALS

Distance: 5 miles (8 km)

Route: Easy; gentle rise leaving Carperby. Ten stiles

Time: Approx. 3 hours

Terrain: Good fieldpaths and firm tracks

Starting Point: Castle Bolton village centre.
Grid ref SE 033 918, postcode DL8 4ET

Parking: Bolton Castle car park, as above

Food and Toilets: Tearoom at Castle; pub at Carperby.
Public toilets at start

Maps: OS Landranger 98 Wensleydale & Upper
Wharfedale; **Explorer** OL30 Yorkshire Dales North/Central

INTRODUCTION

This walk ambles around the gentle countryside of lower Wensleydale, linking a majestic castle with a lovely village.

While the outward leg wanders through a series of sheep pastures, the return takes a slightly elevated route through more open countryside, in springtime much favoured by ground-nesting birds such as curlew and lapwing whose haunting calls are often in evidence. For virtually the entire walk, the celebrated Wensleydale landmark of Penhill dominates the scene across the valley.

A manmade Wensleydale landmark is the majestic Bolton Castle, a fourteenth century manor house converted into a castle by Richard, the 1st Lord Scrope. Mary, Queen of Scots was a famous guest, being imprisoned here from 1568 to 1569, and its labyrinthine interior is well worth exploring. Other attractions include falconry displays, wild boars and neat gardens, as well as special events. Parking charges are refunded for castle visitors.

Though overshadowed by its castle, Castle Bolton village is appealing in its own right. A spacious green divides rows of cottages, many of which housed lead miners. St Oswald's Church stands almost at the castle wall and dates back more than six hundred years.

Carperby is one of the most attractive villages in Wensleydale, its former importance evidenced by the market cross of 1674 set on tiered steps at one end of the narrow green. At the opposite end a group of old chapels include a Methodist Chapel of 1820, a Wesleyan Chapel of 1880 and a Friends' Meeting House of 1864. The Wheatsheaf was the honeymoon hotel of Alf Wight, better known as James Herriot, many of whose popular veterinary adventures were based around this area and neighbouring Swaledale. The characterful Wensleydale breed of sheep was supposedly first named here.

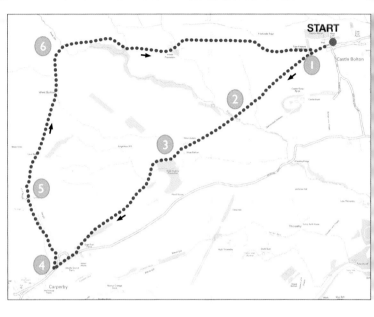

ROUTE

1. From the car park, pass through a gate on an access track into the small field by the castle walls. Cross to a stile in the corner and pass through the bottom of a wood to a gap-stile. Head across pastures, slanting down to a fence-stile then down again to another. Advance beneath a wall corner to a stile by a gate in a wall ahead, then down to a footbridge over Beldon Beck.

2. A path slants right up to a hidden wall-stile, then along two fields to West Bolton. Pass left of the house to a gate onto the driveway, going left past renovated buildings. At the end, as the access road swings left take a wall-stile in front. A track runs to a gate ahead.

3. A track rises to the top edge of West Bolton Plantation, at the end of which is a small gate. A path heads through rougher pasture to a pair of clapper-style bridges, resuming on the other side to a stile ahead. Keep ahead with a fence right, rising gently to a gate at the end. Continue past a barn to another gate and a track through a long enclosure. The track veers to the far left corner above a wooded bank, then slants down towards East End Farm. Pass left of an isolated barn and along to a stile onto the road, turning right to enter Carperby.

4. Return by turning right up Hargill Lane before the village hall. This rises out of the village to become a broad, walled track. A little beyond a barn it starts to climb, and as it swings left in front of an old limekiln, instead fork right on a grassier track.

5. The way runs to a gate at the far corner into a large rough pasture. A green track runs through Bolton West Park; keep left on the main way at a very early fork. After a gate at the far end, bridge Beldon Beck for a second time.

6. After the bridge the track runs through a pasture by the right-hand wall. Go through a gate just short of the corner – not the corner gate itself. The track runs above the beck before passing through a gate in the left-hand corner to follow a wall to farm buildings. Continue on the access track through several fields towards Bolton Castle; passing through woodland the track leads to the castle walls and the start.

8. BURNSALL

THE ESSENTIALS

Distance: 2¾ miles (4.4 km)

Route: Mostly easy; one steep field at the start. Eight stiles

Time: Approx. 1½ hours

Terrain: Riverbank and fieldpaths, country lanes

Starting Point: Burnsall village centre. **Grid ref** SE 032 611, postcode BD23 6BS

Parking: Burnsall village car park, as above

Food and Toilets: Pub, tearoom and public toilets at start and in Hebden

Maps: OS Explorer 2 (Yorkshire Dales South/West); OS Landranger 98 (Wensleydale and Upper Wharfedale)

INTRODUCTION

Burnsall's setting is near perfection, with bridge, green, maypole, church, inn and cottages fusing together into a memorable Wharfedale scene.

St Wilfred's Church dates largely from the fifteenth century, and alongside is the village school, founded in 1602 as one of the earliest grammar schools. Along with the Red Lion Inn, the Devonshire Fell Hotel overlooks the village. An locally renowned annual event is the Burnsall Feast Sports, which take place in August. While numerous events are staged on the village green, the major highlight is the fell race which climbs steeply through the heather to the crest of Burnsall Fell, for the runners to return at breakneck pace down the rough slopes.

The River Wharfe is stunning hereabouts, especially at Loup Scar on the edge of the village where the Wharfe rushes through an impressive limestone fault; in summer you might see teenage boys engaging in foolhardy acts of bravado by leaping into the river. Your walk joins the river further upstream at the exhilarating Hebden suspension bridge. This celebrated its centenary in 1985, having been constructed to replace the stepping stones of Hebden Hippings, which themselves have since been restored to provide an alternative crossing when the river is sufficiently calm.

Hebden is a small village divided by the Grassington-to-Pateley Bridge road. North of the road is Town Hill, a photogenic grouping of attractive cottages and an old bridge. The village pub, the Clarendon, shares refreshment duties with a tearoom in the old school. When the modest St Peter's Church was built it saved the parishioners the walk to Linton church. Hebden, like its bigger neighbour Grassington, grew with the once thriving lead mining industry, with Hebden Gill, and above it Grassington Moor, abounding in evocative reminders of those hard days.

8. BURNSALL WALK

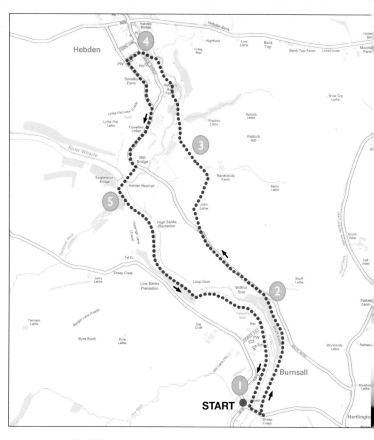

ROUTE

1. Cross the bridge and immediately take a gap on the left to descend sixteen steep steps to the Wharfe. Head upstream through an stile, and on to a ladder-stile in a wall. Here the path forks; your route climbs left above the wooded bank of the river. Crossing a fence-stile, a good path traverses above the wooded bank. At the end it swings round by a sidestream to a stile onto narrow Skuff Road.

2. Go left along here for a while, as far as a stile on the right as the road bends and starts to drop. Go over the stile and cross the field, bearing gently right to a stile where fence and wall meet. Turn right on the drive to Ranelands; on entering the farmyard take a gate left of the house. Drop diagonally down the field towards the far corner, with a gateway alongside a wall-stile. From another stile just behind you overlook the side valley of Hebden Beck.

3. Drop onto a cart track, and go right to a track junction in front of a fishery. Here cross a stone slab on a tiny stream, and a path heads away beneath the fishery to a footbridge on Hebden Beck just ahead, beneath a weir. Across, walk upstream, through a kissing-gate and on as far as a wall-stile. Just beyond, ignore a footbridge and instead follow the main path rising away, curving up to a kissing-gate onto the street in Hebden alongside the old school.

4. Cross to a narrow lane opposite, and continue to a T-junction alongside the church. Here go left on Back Lane, which drops past a farm. Ignoring a right branch, descend between walls to emerge onto the road. Turn down this and head for the suspension footbridge on the river just ahead. Take a small gate on the right to the riverbank, passing through another small gate in the adjacent wall part-way along.

5. Cross the suspension footbridge and turn downstream to return to Burnsall on a popular path along this part-wooded riverbank.

6. This section peaks near the end as you climb a small knoll looking down on the limestone walls of Loup Scar. The final stage shadows the river as it curves round back into the village.

9. BOLTON ABBEY

THE ESSENTIALS

Distance: 4¼ miles (6.8 km)

Route: Mostly easy; undulating paths in and out of the woods. No stiles

Time: Approx. 2½ hours

Terrain: Riverbank and well-maintained woodland paths

Starting Point: Bolton Abbey village centre.
Grid ref SE 071 539, postcode BD23 6EX

Parking: Village car park, as above

Food and Toilets: Refreshments at start, and at Cavendish Pavilion and Bolton Bridge en route. Public toilets at start and at Cavendish Pavilion

Maps: OS Explorer 2 (Yorkshire Dales South/West);
OS Landranger 104 (Leeds, Bradford and Harrogate)

INTRODUCTION

Bolton Abbey is the most popular attraction in Wharfedale. The imposing ruin is a magnet for nearby West Yorkshire visitors, with the River Wharfe an attraction in its own right.

Strictly speaking, Bolton Abbey is the name of the tiny village whose showpiece is more correctly Bolton Priory. The priory dates from 1154 and was built by Augustinian canons who moved here from nearby Embsay. At the Dissolution the nave was spared, and functions as the parish church to this day. There is much else of interest in the vicinity, including the adjacent Bolton Hall dating from the seventeenth century. At the start of the walk are a post office/shop, tearoom, antiquarian bookshop and a large and splendid example of a tithe barn. An archway over the road carried an aqueduct supplying water to a former mill.

The Cavendish name features prominently hereabouts, as this is the family name of the Dukes of Devonshire, long-time owners of the Bolton Abbey estate but even better known for their family seat at Chatsworth in Derbyshire. The Cavendish Memorial Fountain commemorates Lord Frederick Cavendish, who was assassinated in Phoenix Park, Dublin in 1882. The Cavendish Pavilion stands at the entrance to Strid Wood and offers all manner of refreshments, with a gift shop alongside. The woodland walks are hugely popular with families, being firmly surfaced and offering some surprising viewpoints as well as 'money trees' – logs into which thousands of coins have been embedded.

The elegant Bolton Bridge marks the Wharfe's departure from the National Park, and the completion of the 1994 bypass at last left this splendid old crossing in peace. The extension of a steam railway from Embsay has seen Bolton Abbey's restored station back in use, situated half-a-mile along the A59 towards Skipton. The sprawling Devonshire Arms Hotel is beyond a delightfully sited cricket pitch; there is also a tearoom across the road.

9. BOLTON ABBEY WALK

ROUTE

1. From the car park follow the short road to a triangular green by the main road. Cross to a gate at the 'Hole in the Wall' and a firm path descends towards the priory and the river. Follow this as far as a footbridge over the Wharfe, but instead of crossing, turn left on the main path between priory and river.

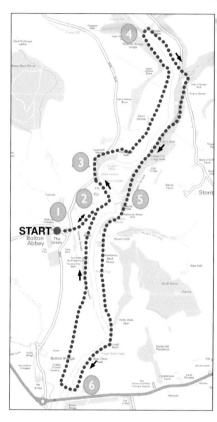

2. This rises to the churchyard above the steep riverbank, then left alongside graves to an access road. Go briefly right to a gate onto the road, and continue for a couple of minutes to the Cavendish Memorial Fountain.

3. Ignore the driveway just ahead, and take a broad path down steps to the right. Emerging into open pasture, descend across the centre to a gate onto the riverbank. A path runs left to meet the car park loop road, which leads upstream to the Cavendish Pavilion.

4. Leave by crossing the bridge over the Wharfe, turning downstream on a path emerging onto a narrow road. Turn right to a footbridge and ford on Pickles Beck, and on the other side leave the road for a firm path bearing right. Coming out high above the river, it climbs again to a major fork just past a viewpoint bench; take the upper path, leading steeply to the very top of the wood. It then runs on to a gate out of the wood. Slant down to a mid-height junction, taking the left branch and climbing back up to rejoin the wood top at a viewpoint.

5. Continue on a path to a bridle-gate, over a footbridge into a field. Follow the fence on your right, then pass through a kissing-gate and go right again with the fence, still above the steep wooded bank. Descend to a kissing-gate into a large open pasture by the river. Continue ahead to a gate at the far end, and a track leads up the wooded bank to a gate. Don't pass through; instead, take a path along the bank top to a gate into another field. Follow the fence to the right above the wooded bank, dropping towards the river. The path swings left towards barns at Red Lion Farm, passing through a small gate onto an enclosed path and emerging onto a section of old road. Go right to cross the bridge.

6. Across the bridge, pass through a gate on the right to follow the riverbank back to Bolton Priory. Retrace your opening steps back up to the road.

10. PANORAMA WALK

THE ESSENTIALS

Distance: 3 miles (4.8 km)

Route: Easy; one steady but sustained climb at the start. Two stiles

Time: Approx. 2 hours

Terrain: Mostly hard surfaced paths

Starting Point: Pateley Bridge town centre. Grid ref SE 157 655, **postcode** HG3 5BD

Parking: Central long-stay pay and display car park in Pateley Bridge, **postcode** HG3 5JX

Food and Toilets: Pubs, cafés and public toilets at start

Maps: OS Explorer 298 (Nidderdale); OS Landranger 99 (Northallerton and Ripon)

INTRODUCTION

Nidderdale is probably the least known of the major valleys of the Yorkshire Dales, due in part to its omission from the National Park in 1954. Belated compensation came forty years later with designation of the Nidderdale Area of Outstanding Natural Beauty.

This is the easternmost of the Yorkshire Dales, and above Pateley Bridge it is a tightly confined valley with high moors on either side. In contrast, below Pateley the dale opens out into a more pastoral landscape.

Pateley Bridge is a busy little town, the undisputed capital of Nidderdale. More a village in size, within its compact huddle are pubs and cafés, an information centre, a riverside park and many individual shops, some hidden down inviting narrow alleys. The Nidderdale Museum contains absorbing displays of life in days gone by, including Pateley's historic industries of lead mining, quarrying and railways. Pateley Bridge is also home to the colourful Nidderdale Show, a hugely popular event that takes place each September.

The roofless church of St Mary the Virgin hides in high-altitude seclusion. Dating from the fourteenth century, its tower was added in the seventeenth. In 1826, however, it was abandoned due to poor access, insufficient size and repair costs, being replaced by the more convenient St Cuthbert's in the town.

The Panorama Walk is a popular local promenade offering easy access and the extensive views that justify its name. Probably the finest feature is the prospect of Guise Cliff directly across the valley from the Victorians' Pulpit Rock, with the two surviving towers of Yorke's Folly silhouetted.

Glasshouses is an unassuming village around a sloping green; the dominant feature is the tall church spire. The village's existence owes much to the Metcalfe family, who erected housing and public buildings in the mid-nineteenth century for workers in their large flax-spinning mill. Glasshouses Mill dates from 1874, boasting an imposing façade with an old clock and large bell. This substantial old mill with an impressive riverside frontage has served myriad operations since its heyday, and currently awaits possible residential development.

Between Glasshouses and Pateley Bridge you walk parallel with the former Nidd Valley Railway, opened in 1862 by the North Eastern Railway. This typical rural branch line ran from near Harrogate to its terminus at Pateley Bridge. The single-track line finally succumbed in 1964, having been closed to passengers thirteen years earlier.

10. PANORAMA WALK

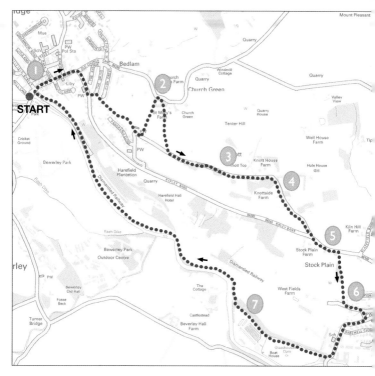

ROUTE

1. From the bridge at the foot of the High Street, head east up the main thoroughfare, swinging right at the top. As the road levels out after the Methodist Church, a footpath sign points up steps to the start of the Panorama Walk. A steep path climbs past an inscribed stone tablet above a well. Immediately beyond the cemetery entrance turn left onto a walled path. Continue along to discover Pateley Bridge's old church hidden in trees.

2. Resume by following the path up the churchyard to locate a wooden kissing-gate in the wall on the right. Cross the field to a gate, and on again to a stile at the end, rejoining the Panorama Walk. Back on the main route the gradient eases and the narrow way continues; an iron gate leads to a viewing platform on a craggy knoll, the Victorians' Pulpit Rock.

3. Continuing, the path levels out to reach the walk's high point at the exclusive hamlet of Knott.

4. Continue on the surfaced access road, bearing right to descend to the main road. On leaving Knott there is a brief glimpse of the communications and early warning radomes at RAF Menwith Hill.

5. A short distance along the footway to the left, cross with care to a kissing-gate just past the last house. A flagged path descends a fieldside to another kissing-gate, from where an enclosed path drops onto a rough lane on the edge of Glasshouses. Turn left along this access road to emerge onto the village green.

6. Turn right along the bottom edge of the green, descending past the former railway station and the school to approach Glasshouses Bridge alongside the former mill. Without crossing the bridge, take the broad carriageway upstream for a dead-flat return to Pateley Bridge.

7. Rejoin the river at a weir marking the start of the mill-cut. Across it is the gaunt mansion of Castlestead, erected in 1862 for the mill-owning Metcalfes. Follow the Nidd upstream on a broad path, with the course of the former railway evident during the final stages before you enter the town.

MORE WALKING BOOKS FROM BRADWELL BOOKS FOR YOU TO ENJOY

FROM THIS SERIES

BRADWELL'S POCKET WALKING GUIDES
10 Walks up to 6 miles,
suitable for all the family

Somerset
Essex
The Peak District

WALKS FOR ALL AGES
20 Walks up to 6 miles,
suitable for all the family

The Black Country
Cambridgeshire
Carmarthenshire
The Chilterns
Cheshire
Co Durham
Cornwall
On Dartmoor
Devon
Dorset
Essex
Exmoor
Greater Manchester
Hampshire
Herefordshire
Kent
The Lake District
Lancashire
Leicestershire and Rutland
Lincolnshire
London Greater
Norfolk
North East Wales
Northamptonshire
Northumberland
Nottinghamshire
The Peak District
The Scottish Borders
Snowdonia & North West Wales
Somerset
Staffordshire
East Sussex

West Sussex
Vale of Glamorgan & Bridgend South
Wales
West Yorkshire
Wiltshire
The Yorkshire Dales

WALKS FOR ALL SEASONS
20 Walks up to 6 miles, suitable for all the
family throughout the year

Lincolnshire
Nottinghamshire

BRADWELLS LONGER WALKS
20 More challenging walks of up to 12 mile
suitable for the more experienced walker

On Dartmoor
The Peak District
The Yorkshire Dales

COMING OUT IN 2017

WALKS FOR ALL AGES
20 Walks up to 6 miles,
suitable for all the family

Pembrokeshire
Suffolk
South Downs National Park
North York Moors

BRADWELL WALKING GUIDES
8 Family walks
Buxton
The Monsal Trail

Available from your
local bookshop or
order online

bradwellbooks.co.uk